POLLY BETTON
Party!

HOW TO ORGANISE
A BRILLIANT BASH:
THE ESSENTIAL GUIDE

K
Kyle Books

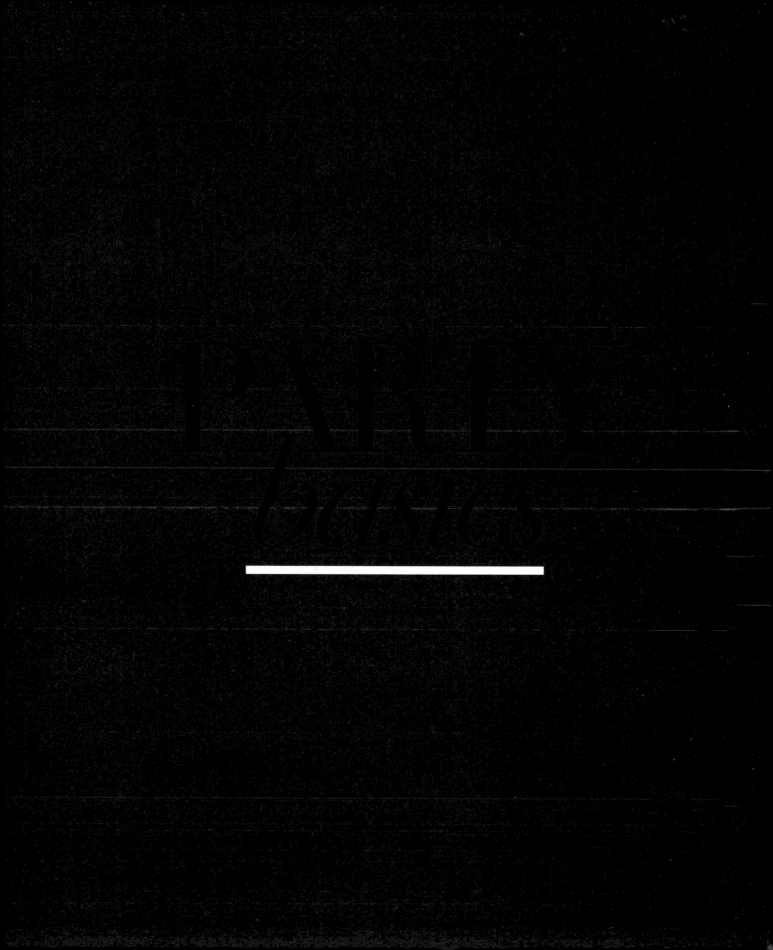

PARTY

basics

DAYTIME
entertaining

Art food

Since your menu will be inspired by artworks or artists, it makes sense to present each dish as if it were an artwork in its own right. Try to light each individually (clip-on mini spotlights are excellent for this, and can be found inexpensively online), and consider the backdrops and props. Some of the items I'm going to suggest work as a direct copy of the artwork, others just reference the form, so use your judgement on how far to go. I also recommend that you label each item with information on the artwork, artist and the contents of your replica, e.g. 'Piet Mondrian's *Composition No. 8* (1939–1942); red velvet cake, natural food colouring, icing.'

Not included here, but worth thinking about if you're inclined to go for something monumental, is a recreation of Wayne Thiebaud's painting, *Cakes*. Display this alongside a colour copy of the painting to give your guests the full effect of your artistry.

Paul Cezanne's *Compotier, Pitcher, and Fruit* (left), Clara Peeters's *Slice of butter on a porcelain plate, on a cheesestack on a pewter plate, with a jug, a wineglass, a bun, crayfish, a knife and shrimps platter* (above) and Antoine Vollon's *Mound of Butter* are examples of artwork you can more or less exactly replicate. Simply buy what you see and create your best approximation with the aid of lighting, fabrics and props.

Rothko trifle

Sponge flan base
(large enough to cover the
bottom of your container
if using a single large one)

Cointreau or other orange liqueur

2 vanilla pods

600ml cream

6 large egg yolks

2 teaspoons cornflour

100g caster sugar

3 leaves of gelatine (always
use leaves, never powder)

150ml orange juice (best if fresh
squeezed from really nice oranges)

200g plain chocolate, grated

This dessert is based on *No.9*, painted by Rothko in 1954. It's not so much a trifle as a lovely custardy dessert, but since it also features a sponge base and a jelly layer I've designated it one anyway. The idea is that the cross section (i.e. the side view if you make it in a transparent container) echoes the colours and proportions of the painting. For the best possible effect, use a square glass. It's just as effective to make lots of little 'Rothkos'.

Start off by preparing the sponge base. This is really easy – just turn the container upside down and press it into the ready-made flan base so that it marks out the size and shape for you. Then cut around the marks – slightly smaller so it's easy to get in. You'll need to do this a few times if you're doing lots of trifles in little containers, since you'll need one for each. Then pop it into the bottom of the container and drizzle it with a little Cointreau.

The next layer up is the vanilla custard. This is really straightforward to make and incredibly yummy. We're actually going to make a double batch and split it to make the top layer of chocolate custard. Split the two vanilla pods and scoop out the seeds. Pop the seeds and the pods into a pan with the cream and heat gently to simmering point (NB: don't boil). Meanwhile beat the egg yolks, cornflour and half the sugar with an electric mixer on a medium speed until pale and fluffy. Take the vanilla pods out of the cream and decant the hot cream into a measuring jug. With the mixer running pour the hot cream very slowly into the egg mixture, then pop the whole lot straight back into the pan and continue to heat gently until the custard is thick and smooth. Decant to a jug to cool. Once at room temperature pour half of the custard on top of the sponge base and set aside the other half. Pop the half-made trifles into the fridge to chill. Wait until they're properly chilled through and the top has set firmly before starting the next phase.

Put the gelatine leaves in to soak in a bowl of cold water. Pour the orange juice into a pan with the remaining sugar and heat gently to dissolve. Once the sugar is dissolved give the gelatine a quick squeeze to get rid of excess water and pop it into the pan. Stir continuously to melt the gelatine leaves. Then take off the heat and add the cold water. Stir to incorporate and pour the lot back into the measuring jug, then set aside to cool. Take the trifles out of the fridge and pour a thin layer of orange jelly on top of the vanilla custard layer. Pop back into the fridge to set – again, wait until the jelly is completely set before starting the next bit. This is really important because if the previous layers isn't completely set the warmth of the next (even if it's quite cool) will cause the layers to bleed into each other.

Next you need to pour the reserved custard back into the pan and heat gently. Throw in 150g of the grated chocolate and stir until it has completely melted into the custard. Pour back into the jug and set aside to cool. Once at room temperature get the trifles out of the fridge and pour on the final, chocolate layer. Pop back into the fridge to set. Just before you serve the trifle sprinkle it with the remaining grated chocolate.

Sandwiches

Sandwiches don't have to be repetitive. It's all too easy to forget that there are lots of different options for sandwich presentation beyond the plastic-wrapped triangle.

Open sandwich: Smoked salmon and dill

Rye bread (preferably a long, thin loaf)

Dill butter (see Flavoured butters below)

Smoked salmon

Dill, to garnish

Slice the rye bread into ½cm thick rounds. If your rye loaf is large, halve or quarter the slices. Spread each slice generously with dill butter and top with a roll of smoked salmon and a sprig of dill.

Finger sandwich: Cucumber and mint

White bread

Mint butter (see flavoured butters below)

Mint, chopped

Cucumber

Cut your bread into slices around ½cm thick. Cut the crusts off, then spread with mint butter and sprinkle liberally with mint. Slice your cucumber thinly and lay out, overlapping slightly, on top of the mint. Place another slice of bread butter-side down, on top. Cut your sandwich in half, then divide each half into dainty fingers.

Pinwheel sandwich: Ham and watercress with basil butter

Sliced white bread

Basil butter (see flavoured butters below)

Watercress, chopped

Thinly sliced ham

Cut the crusts off your white bread and then make it as flat as possible with a rolling pin. Spread with basil butter and layer with watercress and ham. Carefully roll up your bread (like a Swiss roll) and wrap the resulting long thin roll in clingfilm. Refrigerate for at least an hour, then unwrap and carefully slice into 1cm thick rounds with a sharp knife.

Triangle sandwich: Egg mayonnaise and sliced spring onion on wholewheat

Boiled eggs, finely chopped

Mayonnaise

Salt and pepper

Wholewheat bread

Salted butter

Spring onions, finely sliced

Mix your boiled eggs with a couple of dollops of mayonnaise and a pinch of salt and pepper. Slice the wholewheat bread approximately ½cm thick and spread with butter. Spread the egg mayonnaise over a slice of buttered bread and sprinkle with spring onions. Place another slice of buttered bread face down on top to close the sandwich. Slice diagonally from corner to corner on both sides and serve your sandwiches as dainty triangles.

Flavoured butters

Flavoured butters are sometimes called compound butters (or *beurre composé* if you feel like showing off). Flavoured butters can be savoury or sweet and were a particular favourite at Victorian low tea. We're all familiar with garlic butter, but not many people know there are so many other options out there. Excellent flavourings include fresh herbs, brown sugar and marmalade.

All flavoured butters are made using the same method: soften the butter and beat in the flavouring ingredients at medium speed until blended. Leave to stand in a cool spot for a couple of hours so that the flavour develops, then shape or press into containers and refrigerate.

AL FRESCO
parties

AL FRESCO PARTIES

An outdoor party is one of the great simple pleasures in life. The picnic became popular in the early 19th century and the general form is much the same today as it was then – al fresco eating in a pleasant setting. An invitation to a picnic conjures images of balmy summer days, bodies lounging on fragrant turf and toes dipped in icy cold flowing water: the ultimate in relaxed entertaining.

Planning ahead

Preparation is the key to outdoor entertaining, whether it's for the disposal of dirty plates or a downpour. Set up a specific point for plates and servingware to be cleared to, with a bin for rubbish, bottles and scraps. Have an indoor option and/or umbrellas and canopies in case of rain, and plenty of soft drinks and parasols in case of high temperatures. There will be considerations specific to your venue, so think through any potential problems and do your best to minimise them.

Al fresco menus

The ideal al fresco menu has the following qualities:

- Served at room temperature, so that you don't struggle to keep it hot or cold.
- Keeps well, so that it can be packed up and transported once prepared.
- Light, because nobody wants to feel too heavy for a post-picnic game or two.
- Mainly finger food to minimise dirty plates and cutlery.

Essentially you need to reduce faff to the minimum. There's no need for elaborate techniques or construction when you've got a beautiful natural setting and great friends.

Unusual locations

The best way to make an impact is to take your guests to a place they've never thought of as a party venue. A little research will reveal a host of interesting and unexpected spots, from farms to luxury boats, lighthouses, tipis or double decker buses. You often need to apply to the local authority for permission to dispense alcohol or provide entertainment in unusual locations so ring your local authority for details. For larger parties it's often most practical to rent out a whole campsite or country estate. Don't just assume that they won't allow it if it's not on the website; ring and ask. Those who are willing to negotiate are blessed with the best deals.

Sports day picnic

The sports day picnic is perhaps the most accessible sort of picnic – perfectly suited to the local park, easy to put together and high on fun kitsch value.

Setting up

You'll need lots of large blankets to make one long eating and seating area. Scatter with big, brightly coloured cushions and blankets: anything from your house that you can bundle up and bring along is good. Parasols to offer some shade, and a battery-powered radio to tune into a jazz station are also great if you have them to hand. You'll need a big bag of tent pegs and some thick white string or plastic tape. Use the tape to mark out the lanes for your races, anchoring it at either end with pegs.

Even in a public space a little decoration never hurts, so bring along some bunting to hang in the trees, some flags or some streamers. Bunting is very easy to make: purchase felt or quilting squares and cut into lots of triangles,

then sew them onto ribbon or bias binding. Flags are just as simple, you just need some PVA glue, coloured tissue paper and bamboo garden stakes. Cut flags from the paper and use the PVA to attach to the stakes. If you like your flags to be rigid you can dip the paper in watered down PVA and hang to dry.

Races

Fun races that don't require lots of equipment include:

- Egg and spoon
- Wheelbarrow
- Three legged
- Space hopper
- Sack race

Buy a big bag of medals from a party supply shop, or if you have a larger budget, invest in beautiful ribbon rosettes (you can even order them with your own text at the centre if you have time). You could even go bananas and knock together a winner's podium.

Red berry smoothie

SERVES 6

500g frozen summer fruits

60g caster sugar

300ml raspberry juice

500g plain yogurt

Your guests will be thirsty after straining past the winning line in the sack race, so make sure you're ready to offer them some nice cold refreshments.

Pop all the ingredients into a blender and process until completely smooth. Pour through a sieve into a jug to get rid of any seeds, then decant into thermoses or bottles. Super quick, nutritious and yummy.

Banana bread

SERVES 8

120g muscovado sugar

½ teaspoon salt

2 teaspoons cinnamon

360g self-raising flour

1 large egg

125ml full-fat milk

1 tablespoon golden syrup

50g melted butter

4 ripe, mashed bananas

handful of sultanas

More of a tea loaf than a cake, this stuff is incredibly moreish. I like it completely plain, but others enjoy it thickly spread with butter.

Preheat the oven to 180°C/gas mark 4. Lightly oil a medium loaf tin.

Mix together the sugar, salt, cinnamon and flour in a large bowl. Add the egg, milk, golden syrup and butter and beat well with an electric mixer. Fold in the bananas and sultanas with a metal spoon. Pour into the loaf tin and pop into the oven for 1 hour or until golden and risen. Insert a knife or metal skewer into the cake – if it comes out clean the loaf is cooked. Allow to cool a little before turning out onto a cooling rack.

Lemon ice cream with a raspberry ripple

SERVES 8–10

6 large egg yolks

50g caster sugar

550ml double cream

300ml whole milk

100ml lemon juice

1 teaspoon vanilla extract

Zest of 2 lemons

300g raspberries

Contrary to popular wisdom, it's entirely possible to make ice cream without investing in an ice cream maker; you just need to have a long afternoon available. Lemon and raspberry make a great fruity combination that improves immeasurably in a rich ice-cream setting.

Beat the egg yolks and sugar in a bowl with an electric mixer on medium speed. Put the cream, milk, lemon juice, vanilla extract and lemon zest into a pan and heat until just boiling. Start the mixer up again and beat the egg mixture while slowly adding the hot contents of the pan. Return the whole lot to the pan and heat very, very gently for about 15 minutes until the custard thickens – it should lightly coat a spoon. Strain through a metal sieve into a bowl and pop into the fridge for a couple of hours. Once the custard is thoroughly chilled you can start to turn it into ice cream: pop it into the freezer in a wide, shallow container. Take it out of the freezer and beat it after 30 minutes, then replace. After a further 45 minutes, beat it again. Keep doing this at 45 minute intervals for the next 3 hours.

At around the 3-hour point you can purée the raspberries and lightly stir them through the ice cream so that you get the ripple effect. Cover the ice cream and pop it back into the freezer overnight. Serve to your guests garnished with a lemon slice, a mint sprig and some fresh raspberries.

DINNER
parties

DINNER PARTIES

A dinner party is so incredibly satisfying to get right; there's nothing better than delighting a few select guests with an interesting menu and plenty of well-matched wine. Interest in unusual dining has increased exponentially over recent years, so why not flex your hosting muscles with one of the parties outlined in this chapter.

Planning a workable menu

A workable menu can save you from spending a whole evening staring at the stove in the kitchen while everyone else has a nice time next door. Equally, it can save your guests from starting to eat at 10.30pm and spending an hour getting drunk between courses. It's a bit of a revelation when you manage it properly, and here's how to do it.

Choose:
● Canapés that can be made well in advance and either served cold or quickly heated.
● A starter where all the elements can be prepped in advance so all you need to do is heat and assemble it.
● A main course that doesn't involve watching it like a hawk for half an hour (*au revoir* risotto), with elements that can also be prepped in advance.
● A pudding that you just need to remove from the fridge and serve.

And have:
● A separate work surface for assembling and plating.
● All of your plates, dishes and serving implements counted out and stacked ready for use.
● A plan and a decent timer, so that you can run things to the minute while you're in the kitchen without checking temperatures and timings in cookbooks constantly.

Clear the day to chop, dice and otherwise prep everything you need. Pop the ingredients into a series of labelled tupperware containers and get all your bits and pieces ready so that on the night all anyone sees is you sweeping into the kitchen and then sweeping out again almost immediately bearing plates of beautiful food. Good stuff, no?

Wine and food pairing

Wine pairing is a terrifying phrase if you're not a wine expert. Find an independent wine retailer that's run by a genuine enthusiast and take your menu in for a chat. Explain the budget and the flavours you're working with and he or she will be able to provide you with a comprehensive list of wine options, leaving you able to serve your guests without feeling like a wally.

If you'd like to have a go at pairing wines yourself spend a little time researching. Wine and food pairing is literally a matter of taste, which means that it's actually quite difficult to get it seriously 'wrong'; you just have to trust your tastebuds. The lists left and on page 73 offer some guidelines to help you in your experimentation.

Red wines

CHEESE: pretty much any red wine will match well with a strong cheese

CANAPÉS: light, fruity Beaujolais is a good match for a canapé, because it won't overwhelm the delicate flavours

COOKED TOMATO-BASED DISHES (e.g. bolognese): Beaujolais, Pinot Noir, Merlot, Cabernet Sauvignon or Zinfandel will all work happily with a full-bodied tomatoey flavour

POULTRY: Beaujolais again, to give balance

PORK: Beaujolais or the gentle, light flavour of a Pinot Noir

BEEF: Pinot Noir, Merlot, Cabernet Sauvignon or Zinfandel

CHOCOLATE: Merlot, Cabernet Sauvignon or Port

NB: red wine is not recommended for mild cheese, seafood, cream or cheese-sauced dishes or desserts

White wines

MILD CHEESE: Chenin Blanc, Dry Riesling, Sauvignon Blanc, White Riesling

STRONG CHEESE: Chenin Blanc, Dry Riesling, Sauvignon Blanc, Chardonnay

CANAPÉS: Chenin Blanc, Dry Riesling, Sauvignon Blanc or Chardonnay will all balance but not overpower delicate flavours

SHELLFISH: Chenin Blanc, Dry Riesling, Sauvignon Blanc, Chardonnay

CREAM OR CHEESE-SAUCED DISHES: Sauvignon Blanc

POULTRY: Chenin Blanc, Dry Riesling, Sauvignon Blanc, Chardonnay

PORK: Chenin Blanc, Dry Riesling, Chardonnay

CHOCOLATE: White Riesling

Seating

If you have more than four or five guests around your table, create a seating plan – it can make the difference between a good dinner party and a great one. Start with your own seat: traditionally you should be at the head of the table, but don't do that if it leaves you miles from the kitchen. If you have a co-host, put him or her at the opposite end of the table so that you can each look after some guests. The spot next to the host(s) should be used for anyone you need to worry about, so that you can include them. Dot your more charismatic, charming guests evenly around the table and fill in the gaps with everyone else, trying to place them according to shared interests or personality traits. Consider splitting up couples: it can often coax people to join in a bit more, although they'll probably have a moan about it at first.

If you have a guest who can be a pain in the bum ask them to help you by bringing out plates or keeping drinks topped up. Try to seat them next to someone who will be able to cope with them, and if in doubt seat them next to you. Or simply consider not inviting them – entertaining is supposed to be fun, so you really don't have to invite someone who makes a rubbish guest.

Table dressing

This is an enormous subject, so I'm just going to cover the basics. Select a tablecloth that will fit the theme of your dinner. If you want a touch of subtle colour use a plain tablecloth and a coloured or patterned runner. There's a limited amount of space on any table and it's easy to crowd out the useful stuff. Thus: tablecloth, napkins, cutlery, glassware, spaces for any serving dishes/spoons, and place cards (if doing a seating plan) should be accommodated first.

Cutlery is usually laid out so that your guests start at the outside edge of their place setting to eat the first course, moving in a layer with each successive course. You should do whatever you find aesthetically pleasing – as long as they've got the right items to hand your guests aren't going to complain.

Some hosts like to provide a glass for each wine that's on offer, others just stick to a water glass, a red wine glass and a white wine glass – it really depends on the quality of the wine you're planning to serve. If you don't want to crowd a million glasses on the table, just put a single glass at each setting and arrange a good selection of glasses on a side table so that guests can change over as they want to through the meal.

Flowers not only bring colour to your table, they bring scent, which can be a mixed blessing. Don't go for flowers that are too strongly scented (e.g. stargazer lilies) because they will clash horribly with the smell of your food. On the other hand, some gentle scents will complement your food. Don't forget that you can incorporate herbs into your arrangements too.

Titanic

Whole books have been written about the last meal served on the Titanic, but you'll probably have much more fun (and be able to move at the end of the evening) if we take inspiration from the original menu rather than trying to slavishly recreate every element. The focus should be on that very distinctive Victorian form of lavish entertainment: lots of courses, wonderful ingredients and plenty of good wine.

Table dressing

Since this meal involves course after course, you need to leave plenty of space for the various items of tableware needed for each setting. Even if you're a master of getting everything completely cleared between courses, people who are going to be faced with a quick succession of dishes don't want to feel crowded in, so don't stuff the table with lots of decorative items. We need to aim for a starched Victorian aesthetic: a pristine white linen tablecloth, which should be lightly ironed onto the table so that it doesn't have any creases, white linen napkins ironed and then folded simply, and the best cutlery you can get your hands on – ideally a matching set. Add a silver (or silver coloured) candelabra with classic cream tapers and a couple of low, round floral arrangements made up of the great Victorian favourite, roses. If you can get hold of any neat little extra items, such as a silver cruet set, it's just the icing on the cake.

Accompanying Drinks

Three of the courses in this section are actually drinks, so we don't need to worry about them. It requires a little effort to match a different wine to each course, but it's worth it for the effect. It's also pretty economically effective if

you can trim your guestlist to either six or twelve, since a bottle of wine serves six, meaning that you won't be left with an excess of wine when you move on to the next course.

As always it's a good plan to take your menu to a specialist wine retailer so that they can advise on specific vintages. These are some options to consider for our Titanic menu:

- A Sauvignon Blanc will sit well with both the Mushroom, Pancetta and Pearl Barley Soup and the Salmon Soufflé.
- Lamb and foie gras will both pair well with a Cabernet Sauvignon or a Merlot, because they will be complemented by a more robust flavour.
- The Peaches in Chartreuse Jelly with Vanilla Ice Cream will match beautifully with a sweet dessert wine such as a Muscat.
- The cheese platter can be paired with either the Muscat from the last course or the red wine from the foie gras course – it's up to your guests' preference.

Soundtrack

Music will set the scene at your Titanic dinner beautifully. The Victorians would have had live musicians of course, but that's because they didn't have the benefit of a stereo system. Have a listen to some contemporary classical music and choose something you think suits the tone:

- Chopin
- Brahms
- Tchaikovsky
- Debussy
- Liszt
- Mendelssohn
- Verdi
- Wagner

R.M.S. TITANIC
APRIL 14, 1912

FIRST COURSE
Hors D'Oeuvres
Oysters

SECOND COURSE
Consomme Olga
Cream of Barley

THIRD COURSE
Poached Salmon with Mousseline sauce, Cucumbers

FOURTH COURSE
Filet Mignons Lili
Saute of Chciken, Lyonnaise
Vegetable Marrow Farci

FIFTH COURSE
Lamb, Mint sauce
Roast Duckling, Chateau Potatoes
Green peas
Creamed carrots
Boiled rice
Parmentier and Boiled new potatoes

SIXTH COURSE
Punch Romaine

SEVENTH COURSE
Roast squab and cress

EIGHTH COURSE
Cold asparagus vinaigrette

NINTH COURSE
Pate de foie gras
Celery

TENTH COURSE
Waldorf pudding
Peaches in Chartreuse jelly
Chocolate & Vanilla eclairs
French ice cream

Followed by fresh fruits and cheeses,
then cigars, port and spirits

Menu

The original First Class Menu, as served on the R.M.S. Titanic on April the 14th, 1912 was as follows:

Not everyone is going to want to eat until they explode, so the trick is to deliver a long series of well paced, small dishes so that a reasonable amount is consumed over a fairly long period of time. It's a good idea to start your dinner a little early, perhaps 6.30pm to be seated at 7.00pm, and tell your guests to leave out lunch in preparation. Our menu will be as follows:

Menu

FIRST COURSE
Oyster Martinis

SECOND COURSE
Mushroom, Pancetta and Barley Soup

THIRD COURSE
Salmon souffle

FOURTH COURSE
Hand cut Lamb chops, Mint sauce
Roasted root vegetables & purple sprouting broccoli

FIFTH COURSE
Punch Romaine

SIXTH COURSE
Seared foie gras with lavender honey

SEVENTH COURSE
Peaches in Chartreuse jelly
With vanilla cream

EIGHTH COURSE
Fruit and cheese platter

NINTH COURSE
Port and truffles

Alcoholic joust

2 parts red wine

1 part lemonade

1 part Campari

Cubes of Cheddar half dipped in chocolate, on wooden skewers

Created by the Futurist artist Prampolini, this cocktail uses a surprising flavour combination, but somehow it really works. It looks and sounds a bit challenging but tastes great – the perfect combination for a memorable dinner party.

Combine the red wine, lemonade and Campari in a tall glass and then garnish with the cheese cubes on a skewer, which can double as a drink stirrer. Encourage your guests to try all the flavours together for the full effect.

Inventina

1 part Asti Spumante

1 part pineapple juice (or liqueur if you can get hold of some)

1 part orange juice

An entirely inoffensive variation on the Buck's Fizz, using Italian sparkling wine and pineapple juice for an extra little kick.

Pour the ingredients into a tall glass over ice and serve.

Dates in moonlight

SERVES 6

Pack of dates

Pack of pancetta

250g ricotta

Squeeze of lemon

Salt and pepper

The Futurist menu calls for dates and ricotta, and we're going to stick to that pretty tightly. You will need some long wooden skewers for this.

Take your dates and very carefully cut in half across the middle (not lengthways!). Fish out the pit and you will end up with two little date 'cups' (cups are somehow a running theme in this menu, as you will see shortly).

Before you get into date chopping in earnest, line a baking tray with some foil and lay out some pancetta. Bake in the oven or under a grill until super crispy, but not burned. Set aside to cool. Once cool, break the pancetta up into shards.

Pop some ricotta into a bowl with a good squeeze of lemon, and add salt and pepper to taste. Spoon the ricotta mixture into an icing bag fitted with the smallest nozzle you have and pipe a small amount into each date 'cup'. Pop a shard of baked pancetta into the ricotta filling and carefully spear the bottom of the date cup with a skewer, so that you end up with your weird looking canapé fastened on the top of the skewer. Present en masse in a vase as a canapé bouquet.

Geraniums on a spit

SERVES 6

125g smoked salmon

50g cream cheese

25g crème fraîche

Squeeze of lemon juice, plus a good pinch of lemon zest

Salt and pepper

Box of neutral/savoury mini cones or cups

Edible geraniums

Sprigs of dill

'Geraniums on a Spit' is most commonly interpreted as a long pastry twist accessorised with an edible flower. The problem with this is that simply laying the flowers alongside the twists is a bit dull, and finding a way to fasten the flowers to the stick is a proper pain in the bottom, especially when you have a whole dinner to deal with. My solution to this is both prettier and an awful lot easier, although it does lose a bit of the literal 'spit' interpretation.

Buy a box of ready-made mini cones, making sure that they're 'neutral' not 'sweet'. These are used by a lot by caterers for canapés and are pretty easy to get hold of – you can even buy coloured ones if you want to get really elaborate. You'll also need to order in a carton of edible flowers – don't worry about sticking to geraniums, just buy a nice box of mixed flowers for lots of colour and variety. You can source the flowers from your garden if you prefer, but please look over the Floral dinner section before doing so.

Fill the cones with a super-simple smoked salmon mousse, which is delicious as well as alliterative. Pop the smoked salmon, cream cheese, crème fraîche and lemon juice into a food processor and give it a good whizz. Season to taste and spoon into a piping bag, then put into the fridge for a couple of hours to chill. Don't fill your cones until just before you're ready to serve them, because the longer they sit around the soggier they'll get. Pipe the salmon mousse into each mini cone, and garnish the top with an edible flower and sprig or two of dill. There are little stands available specifically for the purpose of serving these mini cones, but it's fine to serve them laid on their sides surrounded by a pretty scattering of dill and edible flowers.

Aerofood

SERVES 6

Aerofood calls for certain ingredients to be eaten while certain textures are touched – the diner eats with his right hand and touches with his left. The simplest, prettiest solution to this is to make small, textured flags from each material for each item, using cocktail sticks. The recipe matches the items up as follows:

- Black olives = Sandpaper
- Fennel hearts = Silk
- Kumquats = Velvet

Fennel

I fennel heart

3 sticks of celery

50g black olives

2–3 tablepoons mayonnaise

Squeeze of lemon juice

½ tin of anchovies, minced

Fresh Parmesan shavings

The fennel will be served as a little pile of crunchy, fresh salad. Finely chop some fennel, some celery and some black olives, then toss in enough mayonnaise to coat without caking, with a squeeze of lemon juice. Pile up a tidy spoonful alongside the olive tower, top with a sprinkle of minced anchovy and a couple of fresh Parmesan shavings and firmly plant the silk flag.

Black olives

150g black olives, or a mixture of black and green

100ml olive oil

12 sprigs of fresh rosemary

I teaspoon fennel seeds

Black pepper

2 garlic cloves

Squeeze of lemon juice

Simply pop the olives into a jar with a combination of olive oil, rosemary, fennel seeds, black pepper, the garlic cloves and the lemon juice and leave to marinate, ideally for a couple of days. Serve in a little pyramid of four olives, with the top olive speared by a mini sandpaper flag on a cocktail stick.

Kumquats

150g kumquats

100g caster sugar

2 teaspoons vanilla extract

The kumquats are deliciously sweet. Slice them into cute little rounds and set aside. Heat up the sugar in 100ml water and simmer until it is dissolved, then add the kumquats and the vanilla extract. Continue to simmer for 5 minutes, then set aside to cool. Once cooled, decant the mixture into a container, covering the kumquats with the syrup and refrigerate until needed. When serving, create a little pile alongside your olives and fennel and plant a mini velvet flag for the final touch.

If you want to make your dinner more eccentric, try presenting your dish to your guests, explaining the theory, and then blindfolding them to optimise the effect of the textures (and make everything an awful lot messier). You may want to provide aprons or bibs. Ideally, the sounds of aeroplanes overhead should accompany this dish (sound effects compilations can be ordered online).

Shrinking violet

Crème de Violette

Champagne or Prosecco

Edible violet blossoms, to decorate

A very pretty pale violet-hued cocktail that's made in a flash. You'll need a bottle of Crème de Violette, which can be purchased from specialist retailers. It's best served in an old-fashioned Champagne coupe, which you should pop into the fridge on a tray for a few hours before use.

Pour a dash of Crème de Violette into the bottom of the glass and top up with Champagne or Prosecco. Experiment beforehand to find your ideal proportions, it's very much a matter of taste. Give it a quick swirl to incorporate, perch an edible violet on the rim of the glass and then serve.

Roasted scallops with bean blossoms

SERVES 6

12 scallops

Salt and pepper

2 tablespoons white wine

75g breadcrumbs

2 garlic cloves, crushed

2 tablepoons parsley, finely chopped

1 tablespoon Parmesan

4 slices of bacon, finely chopped

3 tablespoons olive oil

12 bean blossoms

We're reversing the usual course order here by introducing the fish before the salad, but the recipes are so delicious that hopefully your guests will excuse the departure. These succulent scallops are roasted in white wine with breadcrumbs, parsley, garlic and olive oil and presented topped with bean blossoms, which are not only delicious, they're also terribly pretty.

Preheat the oven to 180°C/gas mark 4.

Season the scallops to your taste and lay out in an oiled heatproof dish. Pour in the white wine. Combine the breadcrumbs, garlic, parsley, Parmesan, bacon and olive oil in a bowl and sprinkle the mixture on top of each scallop in a pretty pile. Put the scallops into the oven to roast – cooking time will depend on the size of the scallops, but it should take around 5 minutes.

Carefully transfer to a serving plate and garnish each scallop with a bean blossom.

DRINKS
parties

DRINKS PARTIES

The elegant drinks party has many advantages over the more raucous house party from the perspective of the 'grown up' host. Quality over quantity is the watchword for this form of entertaining, from your guestlist to your food offering – it's a great opportunity to take pleasure in the details.

Putting together a soundtrack

Music can instantly transport you to an entirely different time and place, lifting your mood and helping to kick-start a memorable evening. It's therefore advisable to spend time beforehand creating a made-to-measure soundtrack. Do a little research on appropriate eras or genres of music. This is pretty straightforward online; most music retail websites will let you listen to a preview before you buy and there are lots of specialist music blogs out there offering advice. Work out approximately how long you expect your party to last, then add an hour and a half – that's how much time you need to fill with your music.

You can create your playlist using a computer with software such as iTunes (which is compatible with both Mac and PC and is free to download). Just drag and drop your tracks into the order you'd like them to play. Consider the narrative of the party as you do so: you need the music to start out fairly relaxed, getting more upbeat at the party progresses and then gradually winding down towards the end. The ideal is to connect your laptop or mp3 player to the sound system – that way you won't need to keep changing CDs – but if need be you can burn your playlist onto several CDs (don't forget to number them) and set yourself timers to remind you when to swap.

Setting up a bar

Setting up a bar is only as complicated as you choose to make it. Don't feel that you have to offer a full cocktail bar to your guests; it's perfectly acceptable to offer a limited but carefully chosen range of drinks. The basic bar offers beer, wine and soft drinks. This means you can make your bar self-service if you want to. If you'd like to offer cocktails you should either choose a single cocktail, which can be a welcome drink, or a selection of 4–5 cocktails, which can be presented in a menu. Once cocktails are involved you need to employ a professional bartender or at least someone who understands how these things work.

Once your menu is fixed you need to work out how much to buy in. This depends largely on your guests; for a big celebration you should allow 3–4 drinks per hour per person, but for a more sedate party, 1–3 per hour is fine. If you want to ensure that you won't run out, allow for an extra hour's worth. You should purchase your alcohol from a wholesaler – they generally offer sale or return (which means any unopened, undamaged bottles or cases will be taken back and refunded after the party) as well as free glass and ice-bucket hire.

Finally you need to make sure you've got all of the accoutrements – corkscrews, bottle openers, lemon and lime wedges, and, most importantly, ice. Since bottle openers tend to disappear, anchor them to the table with a long piece of string. You also need to set up several prominent bins.

Film noir

This is not only an incredibly stylish drinks party theme, it's also perfectly suited to the pace of this type of entertaining. Your guests can pull out all the stops on the glamour front without worrying about getting sweaty dancing or being able to eat a lot. Plus of course the tropes of film noir are ripe for a little tongue-in-cheek humour, so you can have some fun with it too.

The ever-fabulous Jane Russell, ultimate film noir heroine.

Film noir backdrop

The obvious thing to do at a film noir party is to show some film noir. You don't especially want everyone to sit and watch the whole thing in silence, so just show the films with the sound off and switch on the subtitles if you think people would like to be able to follow the narrative. There are a couple of different ways of displaying the films – if you've got a TV *in situ* then it's fine to just play the DVDs on that. If you have a little more time and access to a projector, it's nice to project across a whole wall, perhaps in the garden – that way you get to see the dramatic art direction of the film noir on a grand scale. If you have access to multiple TVs then set up several screens around your party venue and play a different film on each one. NB: you don't want to end up with the dreaded blue screen so set yourself timers to remind you when a film is ending so that you can do a quick swap. Films to consider showing include:

- *Der Blaue Engel (The Blue Angel)*, 1930, Josef von Sternberg
- *Citizen Kane*, 1941, Orson Welles
- *Stranger on the Third Floor*, 1940, Boris Ingster
- *The Lost Weekend*, 1945, Billy Wilder

Double bluff: Poker school

A favourite setting of the film noir is the gambling joint, so it makes sense to put together a poker school. Kits that include a felt table cover, cards, chips, dice and instructions can be bought relatively cheaply. If you don't think your guests know how to play poker, type up a simple explanation using the instructions that come with the box, format it nicely, print and display. Include chocolate cigars, visors and toy guns to complete the look. If you're feeling mischievous you can also include a few tips on cheating and some trick items for the enterprising to employ. It's not a film noir without a little double crossing, after all.

Usherettes

A film-themed party is the natural habitat of the usherette. Simply supply your waiting staff with jauntily-angled hats (from your local costume shop) and usherette trays. The usherette trays are very easily to make: you need several identical wooden trays with high sides and handles, and a length of very wide ribbon (from the haberdashers). Tie a length of the ribbon to the handles at either end and use as a neck strap. Your usherettes can then serve canapés and drinks in style.

Whisky tasting

The private eyes in film noir know there's only one real drink: whisky. What's better than whisky? Lots of whisky: and thus a tasting should be incorporated into your event. I'm using the word 'tasting' in the loosest possible sense, because there's no need for your guests to go in for all of the face pulling, loud slurping and spitting involved in a more formal tasting. On this occasion we're just going for a little informed sipping so that people can compare and contrast.

Blue cheese-stuffed endive leaves

SERVES 10–15

4 endive heads

200g blue cheese

90g toasted chopped pecans

I large pear, finely diced

2 tablespoons sherry vinegar

2 tablespoons thyme, chopped small

These take a moment to put together, look brilliant and taste even better – the perfect party food!

Pull apart two of the endive heads so that you've got lots of separate leaves, and set aside. Chop the remaining two endive heads finely and combine with the cheese, pecans and pear in a mixing bowl. Add the sherry vinegar and the thyme and stir gently. Pack the cheese mixture into the endive leaves and garnish with a little salt and pepper, and a sprig of thyme.

Cucumber caviar bites

SERVES 10–15

I cucumber

150ml crème fraîche

Fresh dill, chopped (and sprigs for garnish)

I lemon

Salt and pepper

A small jar of caviar

Fresh, clean and light, these cucumber bites serve up a salty shot of contrasting flavours.

Cut the cucumber into 2cm thick slices (leave the peel on). Scoop out most of the seeds from the middle, leaving the bottom of each slice intact.

In a bowl, mix together the crème fraîche, the dill, and a squeeze of lemon juice, with salt and pepper to taste. Fill the hole in each slice with a teaspoonful of the crème fraîche mixture and top with a small dollop of caviar. Garnish with a small sprig of dill and serve with lemon wedges.

Glow-in-the-dark

First off, let's be clear – a glow-in-the-dark party does not have to be conducted entirely in pitch black, so don't worry about people impaling themselves on the coat stand while trying to find the loo. Secondly, glow-in-the-dark doesn't mean that you have to employ the aesthetic of a raver hippie: just because it glows doesn't mean it has to be fashioned into dreadlocks and/or an astrological symbol while accompanied by a thumping bassline. The theme is actually a great excuse to completely transform the space you're working with, while employing a little simple science to impress your guests. It can look rather slick when done right, provided you acknowledge and embrace the kitsch factor.

Black lights

The key to your party is black light. Black light bulbs produce a visible purple-ish glow, and non-visible ultraviolet light (not the sort that gives you sunburn). Ultraviolet light makes white things (like teeth and t-shirts), fluorescent things and certain organic things glow. Black lights are easily bought online – you can either buy bulbs, replacing all the normal ones in the house for the evening, or you can buy fluorescent tubes, which look a bit more sculptural and dramatic.

Once you've got your black lights you need to work out what you want visible and what you don't. Block out anything you don't want to be seen by draping it in dark fabric. Make sure it's clean – all the dust that doesn't stand out in normal light will show up like a sore thumb under black light.

Glowing decorations

An excellent start for any party is the introduction of balloons. White balloons will glow under black light, and since it'll be quite a graphic effect, it's a good idea to go for a larger, completely round balloon (such as the Qualatex 16 inch). You could use a bit of helium to suspend the balloons in midair, anchored by some fishing line (be careful not to do this somewhere your guests could wander through, becoming entangled). Even better is to use completely transparent balloons with a glowstick inside, which gives a much more interesting effect.

Another bargain – but very graphic – effect can be created using just a ball of string. Use the whitest you can find (some sort of synthetic parcel string would be optimal), and find an empty spot (between stair banisters is perfect). Just wind your string back and forth in long, straight lines to create a mini-installation that will glow under the black light, highlighting the dimensions of the space you've used. This looks amazing when done over a stair banister that goes up several floors, for example.

It's also worth considering using drapes to define your space a little – transparency is a little more sophisticated in this context, so use a fine white mesh fabric to drape over a few fittings or items of furniture. Plus, of course, any all-white decoration will be very effective, from bunting to confetti.

Floral decorations are the perfect way to give glow-in-the-dark a grown-up twist, since white flowers will glow super-white, green leaves will glow red and tonic water can be added to the water in the vase to make it glow blue-white. Whether large, traditional arrangements in white urns or a few artfully arranged leaves and blooms submerged in a transparent glass vase, flowers will pack quite a visual punch.

Glowing cocktails

Glow-in-the-dark glasses and straws are easily found on the internet, but you don't have to invest in lots of new stuff when you can get a great effect from things you already have in your cupboard.

Glowing ice cubes

Quinine glows in the dark, and the best edible source of quinine is good old-fashioned tonic water. You can use any brand, light or regular, just check the label to make sure it contains quinine. Make a 50:50 mix of tonic and water, pour into ice-cube trays and freeze. The resulting ice cubes will glow under black light and are safe to eat. They will taste like tonic water, however, so it's best to serve them in drinks that won't be ruined by that flavour.

Salt rims

Salt will glow in black light because it's so white, so giving your glasses a salt rim is a good glow-in-the-dark option. Run a lemon wedge around the rim of your glass to

moisten it, pour a little salt into a saucer and dip the rim in – the salt will stick to the lemon juice, creating a pretty, frosty edge on the glass. You can do the same with caster or icing sugar if the drink you're serving doesn't suit salt.

Light-up cocktail fountain

This is the sort of thing that can either be totally tacky or utterly brilliant, depending on the setting. In the context of a glow-in-the-dark party, it's definitely the latter. You can find cocktail fountains very cheaply on the internet, and most of them will also light up. Simply fill with your chosen cocktail, chuck in a couple of glowing ice cubes for good measure and set it running – your guests will laugh their socks off (in a good way).

Glowing canapés

Food that contains chlorophyll will glow red under black light – that means any green leafy vegetable such as spinach, swiss chard, mustard greens, lettuce, broccoli and salad greens. Add this to white foods such as cauliflower, radishes or cheese – which will glow white – and you'll have quite an arresting effect.

White chocolate truffles

SERVES ABOUT 12

300g white chocolate, chopped

3 tablespoons double cream

75g salted butter, diced

1 teaspoon vanilla extract

Icing sugar, to coat the truffles

Stir together 100g of the white chocolate, the cream and the butter in a heatproof bowl. Place the bowl over a pan of simmering water until the chocolate is melted and the mixture is well combined. Take off the heat and stir in another 100g of white chocolate and the vanilla extract – continue to stir until the chocolate is melted. Transfer the mixture into a fresh bowl, cover and refrigerate the chocolate mixture until its firm enough to scoop (at least a couple of hours).

Once the mixture is nice and firm, remove the bowl from the fridge and scoop out into roughly 2–3cm balls using a teaspoon or melon baller. Roll in your palms to firm them up and set aside on a tray.

Line a baking tray with greaseproof paper and lay out two forks. Melt the remaining 100g of white chocolate in a bowl over a pan of simmering water. Keep the temperature very low because white chocolate is inclined to dry out and burn very quickly. Take a ball and drop it into the melted chocolate. Quickly fish the ball out of the chocolate using a fork and carefully place onto the greaseproof paper. Set aside to cool and harden, repeat for each truffle.

NB: don't refrigerate the truffles as it will give the chocolate a dull finish. Once they are fully set, dust the truffles with icing sugar and serve.

HOUSE
parties

Cheese and pineapple hedgehog

We all remember (fondly or with a shudder) the cheese and pineapple hedgehog from childhood birthday parties. Think of it as a weirdly presented cheeseboard and it suddenly seems a perfectly reasonable proposition. Avoid torturing your guests with sweaty Cheddar and pop some of the following combinations onto cocktail sticks instead:

- Torn mozzarella wrapped in prosciutto and a basil leaf with a small squirt of balsamic glaze.
- Thinly sliced quince jelly, thinly sliced Brie and thinly sliced pear.
- A small cube of goat's cheese with a couple of blueberries.
- Half a strawberry, hulled and filled with any blue cheese.
- Ripe quartered figs with a smear of Stilton and a light drizzle of honey.
- Fresh or dried apricot slices with little wedges of Camembert.

Halve a grapefruit (or a melon if you want to fit more 'spines' on), wrap in foil and spear with your yummy cocktail-sticked morsels.

Truffle popcorn

Butter

Truffle oil

Parsley

Parmesan

Truffle salt

1 packet of popcorn kernels

A lovely grown-up twist on the traditional movie-goers' snack. Allow 50g popped corn per person.

First melt down a knob of butter, mix in a good splash of truffle oil and set aside. Finely chop a couple of sprigs of parsley, then mix in with some grated Parmesan and a couple of pinches of truffle salt and set aside in another bowl. Pop the corn kernels in a pan as per the packet instructions, replacing half the oil with truffle oil. Once the popping has stopped, put the popcorn into a large metal bowl and toss with the butter and oil mixture. Then sprinkle over the cheese, salt and parsley mixture and toss again. Do this in small batches if you're making a lot of popcorn so that the whole lot is thoroughly flavoured. Try not to eat the lot before your guests get to it.

Naughty biscuits

SERVES ABOUT 20

125g softened unsalted butter

100g caster sugar

A pinch of salt

1 egg

125g plain flour

125g self-raising flour

A little milk

This one's good for a giggle. As a child you may have encountered 'Nice' biscuits. If not, let me enlighten you: these small rectangular biscuits have pretty scalloped edges, a dusting of sugar and the word 'Nice' firmly imprinted into them. It's impossible to stop eating them once you've started. Here I've reworked the Nice biscuits into Naughty ones. For this you will need a scalloped, rectangular biscuit cutter (or any biscuit cutter you like really) and a cookie letter stamp set (a set of plastic letters that can be clipped together to imprint words onto biscuits).

Preheat the oven to 180°C/gas mark 4.

Put the butter and sugar in the bowl of an electric mixer and beat on medium speed until soft and creamy. Add the salt and the egg and mix again. While the mixer is still running, gradually add the flour until it's all mixed in. If the mixture is a bit dry, add a little milk to soften it (but only if it's not sticking together properly as you don't want a gooey mess).

Take the mixture from the bowl and plop onto a floured surface. Knead lightly until it stops sticking to your fingers and starts sticking to itself. Roll the dough out to around 6mm-thick, and cut out nice little biscuits with the biscuit cutter. Ruin everything by stamping rude words into them, firmly so that they don't warp during baking. I like to write 'bugger off' on mine, but do feel free to use whatever expletives are closest to your black little heart. Dust with caster sugar and bake for 8 minutes. Keep them in longer if you prefer a crunchier biscuit, shorter if you want them more raw.

Popping chocolate rice crispy cakes

SERVES ABOUT 20

200g dark chocolate
(the best quality you can find)

1 teaspoon ginger

1 teaspoon freshly grated nutmeg

200g popping candy
(either from a sweet shop, or a
specialist supplier of molecular
gastronomy ingredients)

60g Rice Krispies

Petit four cases
(the super tiny ones)

Coloured sugar sprinkles
(to decorate)

I have to concede that giving rice crispy cakes an extra popping element doesn't make them much more sophisticated. It does make them quite a lot more fun, though, and using excellent-quality chocolate goes some way to mitigate the childishness of feeding an unsuspecting guest a sober looking treat that then goes 'bang' in his or her mouth. Because popping candy gradually loses it's 'pop' when exposed to moisture, it's best to make these the day they're going to be served.

Melt the chocolate in a bowl over simmering water. NB: watch it like a hawk, because the darker the chocolate, the more likely it is to burn. Stir continuously and keep the heat very low. Once the chocolate is melted, pour into a larger bowl and add the ginger and nutmeg, followed by the popping candy and the Rice Krispies. Mix together until well coated with chocolate and carefully spoon little dollops into the petit four cases. Top with a few sugar sprinkles and refrigerate until set. Serve to your guests with quiet glee.

Colourscape

This is a theme that works for all ages, from children's parties to grown up psychedelic extravaganzas. The premise is simple: colour, piles and piles of vibrant, exciting colour. It needs to be all-out in the execution; this is not a theme for the faint-hearted. Colourscape lends itself to some wonderful dressing up, in head-to-toe monochromatic outfits, and is one of the rare parties that is easy to dress up for without buying anything new or feeling too outlandish.

Since you're probably not all that keen on re-painting the rooms in your house, this party calls for some smart set dressing. As per usual, I'm going to recommend coloured lightbulbs and/or lighting gels as a starting point. Ideally, you should assign an area to each of the seven colours of the rainbow and light it accordingly. Because this party is light and bright you should tint your overhead lighting rather than using lamps.

Balloon room

One of my absolute favourite party props is the humble balloon. They are cheap to buy in bulk, easy to assemble and available in all sorts of shapes, not to mention sizes, ranging from 20cm to over 2m. Fill with helium and you'll have props that add both height and volume to the room. When using balloons, more is more: for this specific theme it's great fun to fill a whole room with balloons of a single colour in lots of shapes and sizes. The pile of balloons should be at least knee-deep (do it in a small room for the sake of your fingers). Your guests will have hours of fun kicking, popping and throwing balloons around, and they will take some great pictures in the process.

Bouncy castle

Now, I know a lot of people think that bouncy castles at adult parties are a health and safety nightmare. But they really are very good fun and if you hire from a reputable operator they can provide someone to lay down the safety law so that you don't have to. Essentially this entails having the castle out when guests arrive and for the first hour or so, with the usual 'no shoes, no drinks on the castle' rules, and then packing it up before anyone gets too drunk and silly. If you really want to cover yourself you can provide signage making it clear that guests use the castle at their own risk and outlining the rules of use in writing. Once your conscience is salved, you will be free to bounce around in your colourful inflatable idyll to your heart's content, and you'll find that it really does create quite a marvellous sense of euphoria.

Rock-and-roll face painting

Parties are a great opportunity for adults to let go of the need to be 'grown up' and indulge in a little play. Face painting is an excellent case in point: it's a simple form of dressing up and make believe that takes people out of their everyday characters. The only difference is that instead of tigers and butterflies, our reference points are Ziggy Stardust and glam rock. You can either hire a professional face painter and brief him or her, or buy a cheap set of face paints on the internet and provide a mirror and lots of inspirational pictures. You'd be amazed at the difference a couple of red and silver lightning flashes to the face can make to your party guests!

Rainbow cocktail bar

At a colour-themed party, it only makes sense to serve a rainbow cocktail menu. Brightly coloured drinks are great fun, and offer a good opportunity to experiment with some interesting liquors and flavours.

Raspberry gin and tonic

SERVES 1

250g raspberries

230g caster sugar

50ml gin

150ml tonic water

Sprigs of mint to garnish

The addition of tart, fruity raspberries to any drink is a very nice surprise. Delivered while you're working your way through an innocuous gin and tonic, it's rather astonishing. Quantities shown for the G&T are for one serving; multiply up by the number of people you need to serve.

To make raspberry syrup
Put about 150g of the raspberries into a bowl and liquidise using a stick blender. Pour into a small pan, add the sugar and heat gently until the sugar dissolves. Strain through a sieve (to remove seeds) into a container, seal and refrigerate until needed.

To make the ice cubes
Don't ignore this bit, they're not just ice cubes! Put a whole raspberry – cavity facing up – into each section of an ice-cube tray. Carefully fill each raspberry with raspberry syrup, then pop the tray into the freezer until the syrup is completely frozen. Once completely hardened remove from the freezer and fill the tray as normal with cold water, then freeze again, so that you end up with syrup-filled raspberries encased in ice cubes.

To make the gin and tonic
Add two or three raspberry cubes to a glass, pour over the gin and tonic and garnish with a sprig of mint. Your guests will start out drinking a normal G&T then gradually get more and more of the raspberry flavour (and lovely red colour) coming through. If you think your guests will get through the drink too quickly to appreciate the ice cube, just make them bigger, stronger drinks to slow them down a bit.

Mini cheese biscuits

SERVES ABOUT 20

250g cream cheese

Assorted food colouring

500g small savoury biscuits
(I like to use Mini Cheddars)

These are a bit of a cheat but they look adorable together on a tray (as well as being yummy of course). A word on the subject of food colouring: the ones you buy in the supermarket aren't very accurate. If you buy red food colouring, the only shade it will reliably achieve is red. Of course you can add less to try to get pink but you probably won't get the shade you want. This problem is easily solved by investing in small bottles of specialist food colouring from a baking supplier. For this recipe, choose red, orange, yellow, green, blue, indigo and violet.

Divide your cream cheese into seven small bowls. Add a little colour to each and beat well until mixed through. If the colour isn't strong enough add a couple more drops and repeat. Lay out your biscuits, load some coloured cream cheese into a piping bag and pipe onto the biscuits in a neat little swirl. Make an equal number of each colour and line up in rainbow rows to serve.

You can also create a multicoloured effect by using disposable icing bags. Fill two or three bags with a colour each and snip off the ends (no nozzle). Take another icing bag with a star nozzle fitted and place the filled bags inside, snipped ends pointing into the nozzle. Twist and secure the tops of the bags with a rubber band. When you squeeze the outer bag the different colours will be forced through the nozzle all together, creating rainbow rosettes. Very exciting stuff, believe me. Don't tell anyone how you did it; they'll think you're magic.

Multicoloured mini pavlovas

SERVES ABOUT 15

For the fruit powder

300g raspberries

300g blueberries

300g bananas

300g apricots

For the mini pavlovas

3 large egg whites

100g caster sugar

A pinch of cream of tartar

200ml whipping cream

100g icing sugar

150g of each fresh fruit (same fruit as used to make powder)

I have always found meringues uniquely difficult to make – I just have no feeling for them. I love to eat them, but every time I try to make them the traditional way I end up with sad, hard little dollops of failure. So I was delighted to hear from experimental caterers *par excellence* Blanch and Shock that I could make them in a dehydrator with no margin for error at all. The traditional baking process is actually more a process of drying out, so it makes sense that dehydrating is just a much more reliable way of doing it. This recipe will make pretty mini pavlovas with swirly stripy meringues, coloured fruity cream and a corresponding fruit topping. If you don't have a dehydrator, just use your preferred meringue recipe to cook the mini pavlovas in the conventional way. Another option is to buy ready-made fruit powder online – Sosa do a good one.

To make the fruit powder

This is a gloriously easy and effective technique, which also makes use of the dehydrator (you may as well get your money's worth). Just dehydrate the fruit overnight (about 8 hours), then blitz in a coffee grinder.

To make the mini pavlovas

All of the equipment you use must be super clean – any hint of grease or grime will spoil things. Give your mixer bowl a quick once over with the cut side of a lemon before you start just to make sure that all traces of grease are gone.

Put the egg whites into the mixer bowl and beat on medium speed until they are firm enough to form soft peaks. Continue mixing on the same speed while slowly adding in the caster sugar, a small amount at a time. Once the sugar is well combined and your meringue mix is starting to form stiff peaks, add a pinch of tartar and mix a little more.

Next you need to add the flavour and colour to the meringues. Doing this is pretty simple – just smear a dollop of the fruit powder onto a plate, and using a metal spoon take a spoonful of the meringue and gently roll it through the powder so it takes on a smattering of the stuff. Then plop it into the dehydrator, make a little hollow in the middle and repeat. NB: you want to have lots of small dollops unless you've got an enormous dehydrator. Once you've made all your meringues dehydrate them for about 6 hours, or overnight.

Once the meringues are all nicely dried out, beat the whipping cream and icing sugar until thick. Separate off some of the beaten cream for each flavour and fold in some of the fruit powder with a metal spoon. Dollop the cream onto the corresponding meringue (raspberry goes with raspberry etc.) and top with the corresponding fresh fruit.

Refrigerate the pavlovas for roughly 1 hour to set the cream properly before serving.

Prohibition

The 'Roaring 20's' is a very popular variation on the vintage party. Of course Prohibition only happened in the USA, but nobody's going to bash you for a few historical inaccuracies at a house party, so don't feel you have to make the rest of what's going on authentically American – just focus on the good bits: gin, jazz and flapper dresses.

Dressing up

A 1920s party brings out the peacock in a chap. Pander to this urge with a selection of disposable dressing-up items for your guests to raid at will. A mantelpiece is always a good spot for this sort of display. Start by investing in two or three polystyrene heads (the sort used for wig and hat display). There are several different shapes to choose from: personally I'd go for a standard male, a standard female and a swan-necked head for variation. If you can beg, borrow or steal a couple of dressmaking dummies or mannequins, so much the better.

Next you need your dressing-up items: wigs (flapper bobs with fringes), feathered headbands, long strings of 'flapper pearls', long gloves, great big costume rings, long cigarette holders (with joke shop cigarettes), bowler hats, cravats, fake moustaches, and a couple of flapper dresses. All these can be sourced from joke shops, second-hand retailers or online at very little expense. If in doubt buy the cheapest, since they'll be thrown out after the party. Quality isn't an issue. Arrange and drape your bits and bobs as artistically as possible and let the free-for-all begin. Don't be surprised if you end up with the men in frocks and the ladies sporting moustaches; it's just the way things work.

Prohibition bar

The Prohibition bar is great fun because it's all about a bit of subterfuge. Drinks should be served in mismatched teapots or teacups. Ideally there should be some clandestine process to getting hold of the drinks too, perhaps a special knock or password to get into the room housing the bar (which should be somewhere odd like the bathroom), for example. Of course a Prohibition bar should serve nothing but the most classic of cocktails: most were invented during Prohibition because the spirits available were too horrible to drink neat.

Silent films

The 1920s was the era of the silent film star – from vampish Theda Bara to physical comedian Charlie Chaplin. Add atmosphere to your party by projecting a selection of classic silent films onto a large, white wall (or a sheet if you're a fan of colourful interiors). Since the films will all be subtitled your guests will be able to enjoy them regardless of the surrounding noise. Films could include:

- *Metropolis,* 1927, Fritz Lang
- *City Lights,* 1931, Charlie Chaplin
- *Sunrise: A Song of Two Humans,* 1927, FW Muman
- *Un Chien Andalou,* 1929, Luis Buñuel
- *The General,* 1926, Clyde Bruckman

If you can get a hold of a pianist and piano or keyboard, a cute alternative is to have a seated screening of a short silent film with a live piano accompaniment.

Food for jazz babies

One has to wonder, what did jazz babies eat? The simple answer is 'not much'. Slender, androgynous figures were fashionable in the 1920s and people went to great lengths to trim off any fat. Canapés first came into fashion in the 1920s, largely due to the advent of cocktails, and then of course cocktail parties. Over the page are a couple of contemporary recipes (note the almost total lack of carbs).

LARGE-SCALE
parties

LARGE-SCALE PARTIES

There are some moments where nothing less than a really big party will do. It can seem a bit of a project, but if properly planned you'll not only have a wonderful time yourself, you'll also have the pleasure of entertaining a wide circle of friends: there's nothing better than making lots of people happy.

Comprehensive planning

Planning, like much in life, is dull but worthwhile. Good parties look pretty chaotic, but that's because the host has a good enough grip on the important bits to let everything else fly. Nothing is less pleasant than an overbearing host, so don't mistake planning for complete control. You can't make people do everything your way, but you can make sure that everyone who needs to knows approximately what should be happening and when.

First, work out roughly how you'd like your party to run. A good start is to fix times for the party to begin and end. That makes it easier to decide when you'd like to introduce food, entertainment and music. Once you've got an outline you can review the evening and choose to add or remove items until you have the right balance.

Next you need to look at the prep on the day of the party. Hire items will need to be delivered, performers will need to arrive and get ready and caterers will need to set up. Try to stagger the arrival of helpers and equipment so that you will have time to deal with each person's needs. Don't forget to ask people how long they will need to set up. Simple things can take a surprising amount of time so it's best to ask the experts.

Finally you need to schedule the prep to be done in the run up to the party. If you want to be super-organised you can schedule your time from the moment you first decide you'd like to throw a party.

Bal Argentée

A luxe silver-themed ball combining futuristic entertainment with good old-fashioned fun. Featuring space age technology, tongue-in-cheek new age practices and a significant dose of serious dressing up, this theme is sure to put the sparkle back in your step.

Decoration

Decorating in silver is a lot of fun, and the best bit is that there are so many silver materials available in such large quantities for so little money. Try for a start: tinfoil. There are some amazing pictures on the internet of whole rooms where absolutely everything has been carefully wrapped in tinfoil as a prank, and they look a-m-a-z-i-n-g. A couple of hours and a little concentration later and you too could have a completely tinfoil-wrapped bar, for example. This has the added bonus of masking whatever is underneath, so you can hide ugly things and botched bits and pieces under a lovely metallic cover-all. You can also make use of traditional decorations, such as the strings of silver beads used on Christmas trees. These are perfect for making an ordinary light fitting into an extraordinary modernist chandelier. Stars are a lovely design theme for a silver party; silver card stars with a hole already punched for hanging can be bought in many sizes from party retailers, and can be hung in constellations around your venue using fishing line.

Liquid nitrogen ice-cream bar

You'll definitely need to find a professional to do this one for you; look up experimental caterers, or try asking a restaurant with a more experimental menu if they'd be prepared to cater it for you. I use London-based experimental caterers/mixologists The Robin Collective. It may sound like one hell of a faff, but the effect is quite arresting.

Liquid nitrogen is extremely cold (hence the need for professional handling), and can freeze pretty much anything on contact. You may have seen science demonstrations where vegetables dipped in the stuff are used to hammer nails into wood. On contact with any item, lots of steam is given off giving a wonderful, dramatic mad-scientist effect. This can be used to your advantage with an ice-cream bar. Your guests will be able to choose flavour options and see the raw ingredients poured into the bowl of an electric mixer. The mixer is set running and liquid nitrogen is poured into the bowl, causing the mixture to freeze while being churned, making delicious creamy ice cream.

Another fun thing to do with liquid nitrogen is to offer Dragon's Breath Popcorn, developed by New York-based chef Marcel Vigneron. Popcorn is incredibly dry stuff, so it's possible to dip it in liquid nitrogen and eat it immediately (it won't burn your tongue as there are no frozen fluids to do so). When you breathe out while chewing, a puff of steam comes out of your nostrils like a 'Dragon's Breath'!

Precious fruit

Fruit selection

2 teaspoons
icing sugar

Edible gold and
silver leaf

A fun bit of *trompe l'oeil*. Gilding food can be a little tricky, so only attempt it if you've got the time and funds! Alternatively, you can use metallic food spray as on page 167.

Choose a selection of fruit to make a central table display. Think about different shapes and sizes, trying to get as much variety as possible. Spread out on a sheet of greaseproof paper.

Work in a cool, dry, still environment. Dissolve the icing sugar in 150ml water. Use the sugar water to paint the fruit with a pointed brush (if your item isn't getting sticky enough just add more sugar to the mix). Use the scalpel to cut off a section of gold leaf, then gently lift the leaf onto the blade of the butter knife. Use the butter knife to carefully position the leaf on the painted area and gently run the fan brush over the surface of the leaf to help it to stick.

Once dry, stack the fruit on a silver or white dish. People will be astonished that the fruit's edible.

—————

White rose cake

SERVES 12

2 boxes of cake mix, plus
ingredients listed on box

450g white chocolate

475g caster sugar

10 large egg whites

900g butter

2 teaspoons vanilla extract

Edible silver balls

A classic vanilla sponge with elaborate icing that will make any occasion special. Because your time will be limited, I recommend taking a shortcut and using a cake mix.

Begin by making the vanilla sponges. I've suggested two boxes of cake mix because you will need to trim the sponges a little before assembly and some cake mixes can end up a bit small. Bake in two cake tins. Once baked and golden set the cake layers aside to cool.

To make up the icing set a heatproof bowl over a pan of simmering water and melt the white chocolate. Remove from the heat before it is completely melted and stir as the residual heat melts the rest of the chocolate. Set aside to cool.

Set another heatproof bowl over the simmering pan. Add the caster sugar and egg whites, insert a thermometer and whisk by hand until the sugar is dissolved and the temperature has reached 140°C. Remove from the heat and continue to beat with an electric mixer on medium speed until stiff peaks start to form. Add the butter a dollop at a time, beating after each addition, followed by the vanilla extract and melted chocolate. Your frosting should be thick, white and delicious.

Trim the top of your cake layers so that they're completely flat. If your cakes have a thick layer of browned sponge on the bottom of the layers, trim those off too. NB: this will destabilise the cake layers so you'll need to handle them more carefully.

Place a cake layer on your cake stand or board. Tear off sections of baking parchment and tuck them under the edges of the cake so that they will catch excess icing but can be removed without disturbing the cake. Scoop a good amount of icing onto the cake layer and spread evenly to the edges. Place the second cake layer – bottom side up to give a good flat surface – and do the same again. Roughly ice the exterior of the cake and pop it into the fridge to set for 30 minutes.

Fit a large piping bag with a large star tip and fill with the remaining icing. To form the roses pipe large, equally-sized rosettes all over the exterior of the cake. Once you've covered the full cake, fill in any remaining spaces with little rosettes. Push an edible silver ball into the centre of each large 'rose'. Remove the baking parchment from under the cake and admire your handiwork. Pop it in the fridge to set for 1 hour or so and then you're ready to serve.

Love

This is an unexpectedly versatile party theme. It works all year round for an engagement or anniversary party, and during February it's great for a Saint Valentine's day celebration. Interpretations can range from saccharine sweet to decidedly dark, but the important thing to note is that whatever tone you set your sights on, there's no need for your party to be predictable.

Lighting

You can set the scene at your venue very effectively with a few small touches. Start with your lighting: soft and flattering with lots of candles and rosy tones.

● Professional lighting gels can be ordered online, cut to size and neatly taped over recessed lighting and spotlights.
● Low-wattage coloured lightbulbs used sparingly are a good way of giving a wash of colour in a room.
● Floating candles and flower heads in large water-filled bowls give low-level light as well as being decorative.
● Tea-light candles in jam jars wrapped with red tissue paper give a rosy glow.
● Red, burgundy, pink or white taper candles in a candelabra give vertical interest and a feeling of luxury.
● Large church candles with small pink, red and green floral wreaths around their bases give both a gentle light and a lovely fragrance.
● If you have a dance floor, and a suitable anchor point on the ceiling (e.g. a beam), it's well worth investing in hiring a motorised mirror ball and a couple of coloured pin spots from a lighting company. It makes an incredible difference.

Budget decoration

If you're dealing with a lot of space on a low budget it's well worth considering making use of paper decorations. Paper chains are gloriously retro while giving a design edge if made from single colour craft paper. More is more in this case, so the greater the swathes of the stuff the better the effect. Similarly Mexican paper banners (available online) are a great way of making an impact at a low cost. A strong graphic option is to hang lots of honeycomb tissue balls of different sizes in a single colour. These can be complemented with round paper lanterns (hire in a paper lantern canopy for an instant effect).

Aphrodisiac tasting

If you're prepared to be a little daring you could offer your guests an aphrodisiac tasting. Don't just serve up the traditional oysters; try out a few of the more unusual 'aphrodisiacs' used through history. Ingredients could include asparagus, mustard, anise, nettles and sweet peas, all of which were popular for centuries. Of course it's best to seek out recipes that include these items rather than offering the ingredients in their raw forms! Don't forget to put together a menu complete with explanations of each of your historic aphrodisiacs and how they were thought to work.

Rosemary-infused vodka tonic

SERVES 1

50ml rosemary-infused vodka (place several sprigs of fresh rosemary in a bottle of vodka, leave to sit for at least five days, strain through a cloth and re-bottle)

15ml fresh lemon juice

150ml tonic water

Rosemary (to garnish)

Rosemary goes well with both sweet and savoury flavours, making it a great cocktail all rounder. The herb is also used to treat depression, so this drink should be helpful for rejected suitors. Quantities shown are for one serving; multiply up by the number of people you need to serve.

Simply fill a glass with ice, pour over the vodka and lemon and top up with tonic water. Decorate with a nice sprig of rosemary and enjoy.

Mini savoury cheesecakes with rose petal pesto

SERVES 20

A handful of rose petals

A bunch of fresh basil

4 large garlic cloves, peeled and roughly chopped

A handful of pine nuts

240ml extra virgin olive oil

2 teaspoons rosewater

100g freshly grated Parmesan

100g freshly grated Romano cheese

1 pack melba toast, ground

25g melted butter

1 tablespoon vegetable oil

3 shallots, very finely diced

450g cream cheese

Salt and pepper

½ teaspoon grated nutmeg

2 large eggs

100ml whipping cream

100g grated Gruyère

Adorable mini baked cheesecakes that are super quick and easy to assemble, given extra interest with a rose petal adaptation of traditional pesto.

Rinse the rose petals and pat dry between two sheets of kitchen roll. Cut the petals into slivers with a pair of kitchen scissors. Combine with the basil, garlic and pine nuts, pour into a food-processor and give it a whizz. While the processor is still going pour in olive oil and rosewater slowly, followed by the Parmesan and Romano. Once thoroughly blended remove the ingredients to a bowl, cover and set aside.

To make the cheesecakes you can use either a proper mini cheesecake pan or a silicone cupcake tray. Preheat the oven to 180°C/gas mark 4. Mix your ground Melba toast with the melted butter in a bowl and spoon approximately 1 tablespoon of the mixture into the bottom of each cup. Flatten lightly with your fingertips (don't go bonkers or it'll bake like a rock). Pop into the oven for 5–10 minutes or until golden brown. Remove from the oven and set aside to cool (don't switch the oven off, you'll need it again in a moment). Then heat the oil in a small frying pan and add the shallots. Cover and sauté on a very low temperature until soft, then set aside to cool.

Using an electric mixer, beat the cream cheese until fluffy. Add salt, pepper and nutmeg. Beat in the eggs, one at a time, and give the whole thing a good mix for a minute or two. Finally beat through the whipping cream.

Fold in the shallots and Gruyère, followed by the rose petal pesto. Mix very lightly, so that the pesto creates a marbled effect. Spoon the filling into each cup so that it's two-thirds full. Pop the pan back into oven for around 15 minutes – ovens vary so test your cheesecakes with a toothpick; if it comes out clean they're done.

Leave to cool in the tray, then remove and set aside ready to serve. Decorate with rose petals.

Lamb, pepper and feta bruschetta with rose harissa

SERVES 20

1 baguette

Extra virgin olive oil

1 small lamb neck fillet

1 tablespoon honey

2 tablespoons rose harissa

1 jar of grilled peeled peppers

1 pack of feta, thinly sliced

Watercress, to garnish

An exotic twist on rose petals, which gives a surprising edge to a classic Mediterranean combination.

Slice the baguette to around 6mm-thick, brush lightly with oil and toast for a couple of minutes either side until lightly golden. This can be done up to 3 hours in advance.

Rub the lamb fillet with honey, and then smear with the harissa. Heat some of the oil in a frying pan and brown on all sides. Cook for around 10 minutes, so that it will be pink at the centre. Remove the lamb from the pan and set aside to rest – this allows the fluids to return to the meat, making it nice and juicy.

Take the peppers from their jar, pat dry and slice into slim ribbons. On each slice of toasted bread, carefully arrange a ribbon of pepper, a thin slice of feta and a sprig of watercress. Very thinly slice the lamb neck and arrange a folded slice on top of each bruschetta for the finishing touch.

Vanilla panna cotta with rose jelly

SERVES 15

Panna cotta and jelly are delicious, luxurious and surprisingly easy to put together.

For the panna cotta

3 gelatine leaves

250ml milk

250ml double cream

25g caster sugar

1 vanilla pod

For the jelly layer

1½ gelatine leaves

1 tablespoon caster sugar

50ml rosewater diluted in 200ml water

Red or pink food colouring (optional)

To make the panna cotta, put the gelatine leaves in some cold water and set aside to soften. Meanwhile, put the milk, cream and sugar into a pan. Split the vanilla pod and add to the pan too. Bring to a simmer and continue to heat until the sugar is fully dissolved. Remove the vanilla pod and either discard, or rinse it, pat it dry and put into a jar of sugar to make vanilla sugar for future use.

Squeeze the softened gelatine leaves to rid it of excess water and add them to the pan (which you should stop heating). Stir until the gelatine has completely dissolved. Divide the mixture between your containers. A pretty way of putting this dessert together is to use extra tall shot glasses, and lean the glasses at an angle while the panna cotta layer is setting. This will create a dynamic angle in contrast to the rose jelly layer that goes on top.

Make sure your panna cotta is completely set before starting your jelly layer – if it's at all unset the two layers will blend. As before, set the remaining gelatine aside to soften in cold water. Put the sugar and diluted rosewater into a pan and simmer until the sugar has dissolved. Squeeze the excess water from the gelatine and add to the pan, heating gently until it is completely dissolved. Add food colouring if you like a stronger colour. Set aside to cool – hot jelly will make the panna cotta layer dissolve into the jelly, making it cloudy. Once cool, pour into your containers on top of panna cotta.

Once your rose jelly layer is set you can garnish each with a single red rose petal and serve.

Pan de muerto

SERVES 20

125g butter

125ml milk

550g plain flour

2 teaspoons dry yeast

1 teaspoon salt

1 tablespoon anise seeds

190g caster sugar

4 eggs

190ml orange juice

2 tablespoons orange zest

Icing sugar

Pan de muerto is a sweetened soft bread baked around the *Dia de los muertos*. It is often shaped into skull or bone shapes and is eaten to represent the circle of life. It's also pretty yummy, which doesn't hurt.

Pop the butter, milk and 125ml water in a pan over a medium heat until the butter has melted and the mixture is nearly boiling. Take off the heat and set aside. Put 165g of the flour into a mixing bowl with the yeast, salt, anise seeds and 95g sugar and mix together. Once combined, gradually beat in the warm milk mixture, followed by the eggs and another 125g of the flour. Keep adding in flour until it forms a soft ball of dough that's not sticky when prodded. Put the dough onto a floured surface and knead for 10 minutes until it's nice and elastic. Pop the dough into a lightly greased bowl, turn it a couple of times so it's well coated, cover and set aside in a warm spot to rise. It should take about an hour and a half to double in size. Punch the dough down and form into simple skull and bone shapes – make a whole skeleton if you've got the attention span! Cover with a tea-towel and return to the warm spot to rise for another hour. Pop the oven on at 180°C/gas mark 4 to preheat.

Once the second rising is done, bake the bread for 40 minutes, or until golden and cooked through. Meanwhile, make up the glaze by putting 95g sugar, the orange juice and the zest into a pan. Bring to the boil and keep going for 2 minutes. Apply to the bread fresh out of the oven while still warm. Sprinkle with icing sugar before the glaze is set.

Quesadillas

SERVES 8

8 flour tortillas

250g grated Cheddar

300g cooked chicken breast, thinly sliced

60g jalapeno chillies, chopped (you can get these in jars)

1 bunch of coriander, chopped

4 garlic cloves, crushed

4 tablespoons sour cream

Olive oil

Spanish quesadillas always contain cheese, but in Mexico they can have all sorts of fillings. They're absolutely delicious, so you'll need to run a bit of a construction line for an hour or so to keep up with demand.

Lay out half of the tortillas and sprinkle with the cheese, followed by the chicken, chillies, coriander and garlic. Lay out the other half of the tortillas and spread with sour cream. Place cream-side-down on top of the dressed tortillas to make a sandwich.

Pop a large frying pan on a medium heat with a splash of olive oil and sling in one of the tortilla sandwiches. Fry until lovely and golden and the cheese is starting to melt, then turn over to fry the other side. Take out of the pan straight onto a chopping board and quarter the quesadilla then serve while still piping hot.

Pastel tres leches

SERVES 12

6 eggs, separated

380g caster sugar

2 teaspoons vanilla extract

220g plain flour

3 teaspoons baking powder

125ml whole milk

1 small can of evaporated milk

1 small can of condensed milk

280ml double cream

For the icing

2 egg whites

A pinch of salt

2 tablespoons golden syrup

280g icing sugar

2 teaspoons vanilla extract

This is – literally – a 'three milk cake', a sponge soaked in three kinds of milk: evaporated milk, condensed milk and double cream.

Preheat the oven to 180°C/gas mark 4.

Beat the 6 eggs whites until they form soft peaks, then add the caster sugar gradually while continuing to beat. Add the 6 yolks and vanilla extract, and beat for another 5 minutes. Mix together the flour and the baking powder in a separate bowl, then add in gradually, alternating with the milk, while still beating the mixture. Pour into a well-greased cake tin and bake for around 30 minutes (check whether the cake is baked through with a toothpick – if it comes out of the cake clean, it's done). Leave it in the tin to cool.

Pour the evaporated milk, condensed milk and cream into a bowl and beat gently to combine. Remove the cake from its tin and place on a serving plate while still warm. Poke a regular pattern of holes in the top of the cake with a toothpick and then pour over the milk and cream mix. Put the cake into the fridge to cool while you make up the icing.

Put a heatproof bowl over a pan of simmering water and add the 2 egg whites, salt, golden syrup, icing sugar, vanilla extract and 190ml water. Beat constantly while heating gently until it reaches a thick, creamy consistency then set aside to cool.

Get the cake out of the fridge and coat thickly in the icing, then return to the fridge until you're ready to serve.

HISTORIC
parties

HISTORIC PARTIES

History is a great source of inspiration for parties, whether providing you with a fully formed theme, a small detail or a certain approach. If nothing else, reading about some of the most ridiculous blowouts in history will imbue you with the urge to produce your own very memorable evening.

The Ultimate Roman Orgies *(c.219 – 222AD)*

The Roman Emperor Heliogabalus, said to have entered Rome in a chariot pulled by naked women (plus a further 600 chariots filled with his stuff), broke the Roman bank with his excessive lifestyle. He would sometimes mix pieces of gold into servings of food (no mention is made of the effect on his guests' teeth or digestive systems) and often packed off his guests at the end of the night with the bejewelled plates and goblets that had made up their place settings. He gifted guests with live animals of the varieties they'd just eaten, new chariots, houses, teams of horses and eunuchs. Heliogabalus was also quite the practical joker, seating guests on exploding inflated cushions, giving gifts of dead flies or propping up unconscious drunk guests among wild animals, which would terrify the guests on waking because they didn't know they were tame.

Heliogabalus' menus lived up to the rest of his lifestyle, including conger eels fed only on Christian slaves, fresh fish carried live straight from the sea in pots of saltwater by runners, camel's feet and honeyed dormice. On one occasion 600 ostrich heads were delivered to the Emperor's table so that he could eat their brains. It's not exactly surprising that working for Heliogabalus could be a difficult prospect – if he liked a chef's new sauce, handsome rewards would follow, but woe betide the chef who created a sauce declared to be substandard, since that's all he'd be eating until he came up with a better one.

The Medici Wedding *(1600)*

The wedding of Marie de Medici to Henry IV, King of France, was an event of enormous dynastic significance, not to mention plenty of pomp and circumstance. But the truly memorable part of the day was the reception for 300 that followed. Hosted at the Salone dei Cinquecento in Palazzo Vecchio, the celebration was designed by Bernardo Buontalenti, a Florentine sculptor and architect. It seems that Mr Buontalenti had a limitless imagination to match his bottomless budget, since it's believed that the banquet featured at least 50 courses, the highlight of which were sherberts of milk and honey, inspired by a French sherbet recipe that was a favourite of Marie de Medici. When guests

The Roses of Heliogabalus by Sir Lawrence Alma-Tadema, 1888.

Dinner in Unusual Places
(1783, 1843, 1853)

While Monsieur de la Reynière was enjoying himself horrifying people, a group of London builders were busy starting another entertainment trend – dining in unusual places. The trend was kick-started with a dinner inside the newly installed golden ball at the top of the dome of St Pauls, which is large enough to accommodate ten people.

The trend was clearly a persistent one, since it's also recorded that in 1843, 14 men sat down to a dinner of rump steak at the top of Nelson's Column, two weeks before Nelson himself was installed. At a height of 166ft, these diners clearly had strong stomachs.

Another notable example of unusual dining came in December 1853, when invitations printed on replica pterodactyl wings were sent out to 22 eminent British intellectuals, inviting them to attend a dinner inside an iguanodon. The iguanodon in question was one of 29 life-size models of prehistoric creatures designed by the sculptor Benjamin Waterhouse Hawkins and the palaeontologist Sir Richard Owen to be displayed at the Crystal Palace. The guests found themselves seated inside the iguanodon's body, being served a fine meal by a team of waiters who had to clamber up and down scaffolding to reach the table. The party rang in the New Year together, no doubt feeling smugly secure in the knowledge that no-one else on earth was doing so from quite such a spectacular location.

The Prince Regent's Banquet
(1817)

George IV (the Prince Regent in 1817) has to be in the running for the title of England's biggest glutton. Which is why we should have a special interest in the greatest party of his time as Regent: the Regent's Banquet at the Brighton Royal Pavilion on 18th January 1817. The banquet was held in honour of Grand Duke Nicholas of Russia and catered by the most famous and costly chef in the world, Marie-Antoine Carême, chef to Napoleon, the Rothschilds and the Tsar. The banquet was to prove one of Carême's most spectacular efforts to date. The evening's high point – among the 127 dishes, including pigeon pies and saddles of lamb – was a 4ft high marzipan Turkish mosque. The Prince Regent was so delighted that he was heard to exclaim, 'It is wonderful to be back in Brighton where I am truly loved.'

Feast of Wild Beasts *(1870)*

On New Year's Eve in 1870, Paris had been under siege from Germany for several months, and food was inevitably becoming scarce. This was an enormous affront to the French *bon vivants*, especially on a holiday. Monsieur Bonvalet, mayor of the third arrondissement, was having none of it. So he organised the *ne plus ultra* of carnivorous dinner parties for 20 of his friends, held at the famous Noel Peter's restaurant.

'But how?' You may cry, since food was hard to find. As mayor, Bonvalet had connections. But not for him the trading of black-market meat: he had friends at the zoo. His guests dined on a menu that included escalope d'elephant with a shallot sauce and roast bear à la sauce Toussenel. The guests enjoyed the meal as only starving gourmands could, and Bonvalet proclaimed his triumph not only a successful party, but also proof that if the siege of Paris continued the solution to the nation's food shortage could be found at the zoo. Paris didn't have time to try this theory out – the city fell to the Germans on the 28th January.

The Thirteen Club
(1880–1914)

The Thirteen Club – named after the belief that the number 13 is unlucky – was formed to refute commonly held superstitions. Established in New York by William Fowler, the club

Interior of the Royal Pavilion, Brighton, 1827.

members attended dinners on the 13th day of each month, seating 13 at the table (the latter point referring to the belief that if 13 sit down to dinner, one of the diners will die before the year is out). The first dinner took place in room 13 of the Knickerbocker Hotel on Friday the 13th January 1881.

The members of the Thirteen Club didn't just focus on that single 'unlucky' number, on their way to the table they would walk under a stepladder and on arrival they spilled salt on the table and put crossed forks on their plates. They ate beneath a banner inscribed *Nos Morituri te Salutamus* (We who are about to die salute you) in a tongue-in-cheek twist.

Naturally, the Club quickly gained notoriety, encouraging its members to give the boundaries another little shove. At subsequent dinners the rooms were decorated with open umbrellas, broken mirrors and black cats. The menus were inscribed on a gravestone, lighting was provided by skull candelabrums and lobster salad was served in the shape of coffins. The Thirteen Club became a sensation, with outposts across the world and over 2,500 members of the original New York club, including no less that five US presidents.

The Thirteen Club was disbanded in 1914 due to the beginning of World War I.

The Vanderbilt Masquerade *(1883)*

Truman Capote's Black and White Ball is seared into the public imagination as the ultimate glamorous party, but it was by no means the only grand event that American society had attended. Chief among these was the Vanderbilt Masquerade, on the 26th of March 1883, which – at the time – was among the most extravagant parties ever seen in America. The attraction of the party was such that even the long-standing feud between the Vanderbilts and the Astors was put on ice. Gossip before the party reached fever pitch,

going so far as to claim that there would be so many valuable items of jewellery at the party that the Communists intended to raid the house. When the guests arrived in their carriages, it's hardly surprising that the first thing they encountered was a large crowd of onlookers keen to see who was wearing what. Fortunately the police were in attendance, holding back the hoi polloi.

Powdered footmen led female guests to a grand state bedroom, which opened out into a fairytale dressing room, a spectacular bathroom and another magnificent apartment in which a little nun sat writing '*bonne soeur de bon secours.*' The ladies gathered in their costumes – Marie Stuart, Lady Washington, Mother Goose, Alice Vanderbilt as 'Electric Light', festooned in diamonds with a head-piece that lit up – waiting for 11 o'clock when it would be time to go down to the party.

Mrs Vanderbilt and Lady Mandeville received guests in the French drawing room, and as the party swelled guests moved through to the grand dining room, then the grand staircase to watch the quadrilles. The first of these was the Hobby Horse quadrille – where the dancers wore full riding kit and cantered down the stairs – followed by the Mother Goose quadrille, which featured characters from the stories, and the Opera Bouffe quadrille – a riot of colour – and the Dresden China quadrille, in which the dancers wore clothing of purest white and powdered wigs. Finally came the Star quadrille, which was danced only by young ladies, each wearing a diamond star on her forehead and holding a wand tipped with a star.

Ascending the staircase to the third floor the guests reached the banqueting hall, which was actually the gymnasium decked out in roses and lined with fabulous floral displays. There they were seated for a luxurious supper. The party continued until well past dawn, with happy guests tumbling into their carriages ready to spread the gospel of

A "BAL DES QUATZ'ARTS" IN LONDON: THE CHELSEA ARTS CLUB BALL IN THE ALBERT HALL

Mrs. Vanderbilt's ball. As an exercise in social mountaineering it was incredibly expensive but worthwhile – the newly rich Vanderbilts were catapulted straight into the upper levels of society.

The Chelsea Arts Club Ball (1891–1959)

The Chelsea Arts Club was founded in 1891 as a meeting place for creatives of all stripes. Artists being a convivial bunch, regular parties were held in member's studios. These quickly evolved – inspired by the Arts' Balls held in Paris – into lavish fancy dress parties at the Chelsea Town Hall, which raised funds to subsidise the Club. The Balls grew so popular that they moved first to the Royal Opera House, and then to the Royal Albert Hall in 1910. A special dance floor had to be put down, creating that largest space for dancing in the world, accommodating 4,000 dancers. The *Illustrated London News* proclaimed it 'the greatest fancy-dress ball ever held in London'. Themes were inspired by the creative zeitgeist, ranging from the Dazzle Ball (a celebration of wartime camouflage patterns) to Venetian Masques.

The parties were huge, but well behaved, until the end of the First World War, at which point the Arts Club Balls acquired (and kept up) a reputation as 'the most scandalous event on the social calendar'. Two artists' models were persuaded to strip off at the 1946 Ball, resulting in mayhem. In later years the police were in regular attendance as fights broke out and it became common for revellers to leave the party on stretchers, having got into too much of a pickle to walk. By 1959 poor ticket sales and safety concerns led to the end of the Arts Club Balls.

A Bal des Quartz'arts in London: The Chelsea Arts Club in the Albert Hall. By Fred Leist, from 'The Graphic', 1910.

Dinner on Horseback *(1903)*

In 1903, Equestrian Club president CKG Billings held a truly outlandish dinner party at Sherry's Restaurant in New York for 36 members of the Club. It was Equestrian Club tradition that each new president should outdo the last with their inaugural party. One can only feel sorry for Billings' successor.

The guests – booted and spurred in full riding regalia – were served oysters and caviar in a small banquet room, where a stuffed horse centrepiece gave a small hint of what was to come. But it wasn't until the guests were led to Sherry's rococo ballroom, which had been turned into an 'English country estate' with a turf-laden floor, a babbling stream, ivy-covered cottages and a backdrop of bucolic landscape, that the full scale of the dinner was revealed. Thirty six horses (which had been brought to the ballroom in the elevator) stood awaiting the diners, clad in white satin saddlecloths (embroidered with the Equestrian Club monogram) beneath specially upholstered saddles. The bridles were heavy gold cord. A 2ft square table was fastened to each saddle, and each horse was firmly anchored in place by a uniformed groom. Menus were made from sterling silver in the shape of a horseshoe. The

One of the surviving images of the 1903 Dinner on Horseback.

diners feasted on pheasant served in feed bags and Champagne served in large rubber casks. At the end of the dinner guests were given solid gold matchboxes and gold-initialled leather cigar cases to commemorate the dinner.

The Last Imperial Ball, Russia *(1903)*

In 1903 the Winter Palace hosted a lavish Imperial Ball, celebrating the reign of Alexei I (the second Romanov Tsar). The 13th February saw a gathering of 390 guests, including 60 guardsmen, all in richly decorated 17th century costumes. The entire Imperial family posed in their finery – which included many priceless original items brought from the Kremlin – before a concert in the Hermitage Theatre, which was followed by dancing in the Pavilion room. The ladies danced reels and the gentlemen a *danse russe*, all choreographed by Josef Kschessinski of the Imperial Ballet.

Grand Duke Alexander Mikhailovitch described the opulent gathering as 'the last spectacular ball in the history of the empire...[but] a new and hostile Russia glared through the large windows of the palace... while we danced, the workers were striking and the clouds in the Far East were hanging dangerously low.'

The Gondola Dinner *(1905)*

The American millionaire George A Kessler was no stranger to unusual parties. Having previously thrown a 'Hobo' dinner (where guests were required to wear tattered clothing and eat out of cans) and an 'Airship' dinner (hosted on an airship hovering over the Atlantic), he had a certain standard to maintain when he decided to celebrate his birthday on the 30th June 1905 at the Savoy.

Kessler need not have worried about letting the side down: his Gondola Dinner is still written about today as one of the most extravagant parties London has ever seen. Taking Venice as the theme, the Savoy

courtyard was flooded with four feet of water, dyed a startling blue to imitate the sea. Enormous painted backdrops recreated the city of Venice, and 400 Venetian lamps lit the scene. In the middle of this astonishing setting a large silk lined gondola appeared to float, surrounded by 12,000 carnations and swathes of roses. Swans swam in the water and white doves flew overhead (not a great moment for the swans or the fish the water was stocked with – the blue dye turned out to be poisonous, killing them all). A baby elephant carried a 5ft tall birthday cake to the gondola, accompanied by the legendary opera singer Caruso singing an aria beneath a large paper moon. The dinner itself was prepared by 15 master chefs and served to the 24 guests by waiters dressed as gondoliers. The evening was later described by Kessler as 'the most novel little party I have given'.

Four years later Kessler returned to the Savoy to celebrate Robert Peary reaching the North Pole in 1909, converting its gardens into an Arctic playground under a blanket of plaster 'snow'. The walls were covered with large white chrysanthemums and the North Pole was represented by an enormous metal nail, ensuring that this dinner, too, was a memorable one.

Parties for Pets *(1905)*

Society hosts in New York at the dawn of the twentieth century needed very little to prompt them to throw a party. Mrs Stuyvesant Fish notoriously held a lavish party for her pet monkey at her holiday villa, and a certain millionaire threw an elaborate dinner for his dog, who sat patiently through proceedings decked out in a $15,000 diamond collar. But neither of these events held a candle to 'Diamond Jim' Brady's party in celebration of his racehorse Gold Heels. The party started at four in the afternoon and carried on until nine o'clock the following morning, during which time Brady's guests ate their way through $40,000 of food and drank 500 bottles of Mumm's Champagne (it would have been considerably more had Brady himself not been

teetotal). The female guests were presented with diamond brooches and the male guests with diamond watches, which brought the total cost of the party to over $100,000.

The Cliveden House Parties *(1906–1942)*

Waldorf and Nancy Astor inherited Cliveden from William Waldorf Astor on the occasion of their marriage in 1906. The young couple quickly put the house to work as the backdrop for entertaining on an epic scale. Fortunately Cliveden was well equipped for the task, boasting horse riding, tennis, croquet, fishing and boating among the many diversions on offer. Cliveden's heyday was the interwar period, when house parties became a weekly occurrence, playing host to the great and good, including Charlie Chaplin, Winston Churchill, George Bernard Shaw, Mahatma Gandhi, Amy Johnson, TE Lawrence, Rudyard Kipling and Edith Wharton, to name a few. By 1939 the Cliveden parties were such a fixture that the regular attendees had been dubbed 'The Cliveden Set'.

A perhaps unexpected feature of these lavish parties was an almost total absence of alcohol – Nancy Astor was a firm believer in abstention. However, in all other areas luxury reigned supreme. Dinners, taken at the enormous table imported from Versailles, always consisted of at least five courses, not to mention the four-course lunches, afternoon

George A Kesslers' guests pose in their custom-made dining gondola in the courtyard of the Savoy, London 1905.

Above: A formal portrait of a young Lady Astor.

Opposite: Sylvia Lopez as Queen Omphale in a still from *Hercules Unchained*.

teas and comparatively restrained breakfasts. Each bedroom was so well stocked that a guest could happily avoid leaving for the whole weekend – iced water, assorted biscuits, cigarettes and smoking accoutrements, the latest novels, fresh flowers (matching the colour scheme of the room) and a writing tray with paper, envelopes, blotters, pens and ink.

Aside from the various sporting activities, the shy (or lazy) could fritter away an hour or two on that 1930s favourite, the jigsaw puzzle. The evenings, when not taken up with eating, were given over to all sorts of games. Cards were incredibly popular among the smart set, as were parlour games such as Charades. Other games afforded a licence to break the rules of propriety, whether in the expression of opinions (the Truth Game) or physical proximity (Sardines). Later the carpet would be rolled back for dancing to the gramophone.

In 1942 Cliveden was donated to the National Trust, and by 1968 – after the Profumo scandal and the death of William Astor – the Astor family had moved out altogether.

The Artists' Ball, Sydney (1922–1927)

The Chelsea Arts Club wasn't the only example of eccentric hedonism – the Artists' Ball in Sydney also raised plenty of middle class eyebrows in its pursuit of eccentric hedonism.

'It was indisputably the most spectacular party that had taken place in the city' – *The Sydney Morning Herald*, August 1922. The Artists' Balls functioned as a platform for outrageous costumes and behaviour. All guests wore masks, which were removed at midnight. The parties were peopled with wild costumes – toreadors and convicts rubbed shoulders with people dressed as famous paintings (Millie Sheldon won a prize for her impersonation of Mrs Siddons in 1923) and Persian princes. Themes were quite often bizarre: the Ball of the 27th September 1923 was a 'Jazz Phantasy'. DH Souter attended as 'King of the Cannibal Isles' with an entourage of female savages and Dulcie Deamer (once officially crowned Queen of the Bohemians) came dressed as a cavewoman and did the splits in her leopard skin costume, gaining instant notoriety. Percy Benison arrived wearing a headdress made from chickens under the title 'Miss 1923'. The 1924 Ball was themed 'Childhood', and decorations included an enormous Noah's Ark, which sat on stage, housing the band. Grown men wandered in nappies, sheiks chatted with angels and 'Miss Australia' did the Charleston. The Artists' Balls were eventually abandoned amidst a public outcry, but were soon revived as the Black and White Artists' Ball, which continues today.

Hercules Unchained (1960)

The Romans were the undisputed masters of excess, so when Joseph Levine wanted to promote his new film *Hercules Unchained*, he took his lead from that well known empire, creating his own modern Roman orgy. On arrival each guest was presented with a laurel wreath to wear and was seated in a room where toga'd musicians strummed lutes. Scantily clad 'serving maidens' and 'slaves' served food from a menu that included 'Noble Peacock in its Imperial Plumage', 'Pheasants of the Golden House Served on Silver Shields', 'Pliny's Chicken in Nests with the Golden Eggs of Crassus', 'Turbot Britannicus', 'Hams from the Herds of Epicurius Served with Ripe Figs' and 'Truffle-stuffed Quail Cleopatra Wrapped in Macedonian Vine Leaves'. Some guests were a little put off their food by the live lion led around the room, but most recovered sufficiently to party into the night.

Alfred Hitchcock's Strange Dinner Parties *(1960s)*

Alfred Hitchcock was a very naughty dinner host. He loved to put people into uncomfortable situations just to see what would happen next. There are two examples:

The Blue Dinner

This dinner gave every outward appearance of being a classic, refined evening: from the gentle background music to the attentive staff. Once seated, guests expectantly watched the waiters as they brought out the first course under silver cloches. Anticipation turned to dismay when the food revealed was entirely blue. In fact, all the food at the dinner was a vibrant shade of blue, from start to finish.

The Place Cards

At another formal dinner Hitchcock found an alternative source of fun – when it came to the time for guests to be seated, there was some confusion over the place cards. As guests repeatedly circled the table searching for their names, it gradually dawned on the sharper ones that their name wasn't there at all. In fact none of the guests' names appeared on the place cards, Hitchcock had deliberately ordered place cards that showed none of the names of the people present so that he could enjoy the awkward moment that resulted.

The Black and White Ball *(1966)*

It's famously said that Truman Capote invited 500 friends and made 15,000 enemies when he gave his Black and White Ball at the Plaza in New York. Thrown to celebrate the success of his novel *In Cold Blood*, Capote's party proved to be the hot ticket of the year, if not the decade. The big gimmick was that while

the guestlist featured only the most famous, beautiful and successful of the day, the dress code stipulated that masks should be worn, disguising their identities (with varying degrees of success) from onlookers and each other.

On arrival guests were surprised to encounter a bank of photographers and gawkers – Truman had quite a knack for self-publicity, and this canny move alone increased the notoriety of the party tenfold as the photos and footage appeared in the national media the next day. Women sported enormous fantasy hairstyles created by Kenneth Battelle to complement their masks, echoing the styles of the 15th century French Court, and men wore pristine black tie. Of course the exceptions were as notable as the rule – Mia Farrow was unrecognisable in a mask, having just cropped her hair into that iconic style for *Rosemary's Baby* and Andy Warhol dispensed with the mask altogether.

Truman Capote stood at the Ballroom entrance greeting guests for two hours before the influx slowed. Guests were shown to their tables on arrival and as the drinks flowed it wasn't long before the dance floor was heaving with frenetic activity. Supper was served at midnight on the dot, to an appreciative audience. By 3am the Ball was losing steam, but many guests lingered before eventually dispersing to late night bars and nightclubs. Truman told the remaining reporters, 'It was just what it set out to be, I just wanted to give a party for my friends.'

Above: Director Alfred Hitchcock eating a giant pretzel at the October Festival in Munich.

Opposite: A masked Gloria Guinness arriving at Truman Capote's Black and White Ball in the Grand Ballroom at the Plaza Hotel, 1966.

Index